The Ultimate Orange Chicken Cookbook

Delicious Recipes and Creative Twists for Irresistible Orange Chicken Dishes

While every precaution has been taken in the preparation of this book, the publisher assumes no responsibility for errors or omissions, or for damages resulting from the use of the information contained herein.

THE ULTIMATE ORANGE CHICKEN COOKBOOK

First edition. January 24, 2024.

ISBN: 979-8224498123

Written by john ahmad.

Table of Contents

John Ahmad

Chapter 1: Introduction to Orange Chicken: Exploring the History and Versatility

Welcome to the world of orange chicken! In this chapter, we'll delve into the rich history and discover the incredible versatility of this beloved dish. Orange chicken has become a staple in Chinese American cuisine, known for its vibrant flavors and succulent texture.

Throughout the ages, oranges have been prized for their tangy sweetness and aromatic zest. The marriage of citrus and chicken creates a delightful harmony that tantalizes the taste buds. But how did orange chicken come to be? Let's take a journey back in time.

Origins of Orange Chicken:

The roots of orange chicken can be traced back to Hunan, a province in southern China known for its bold and spicy flavors. The traditional dish, called "Dried Orange Peel Chicken," featured tender pieces of chicken stir-fried with dried orange peels and a medley of aromatic spices.

However, it was in the 1980s, when Chinese American chefs in the United States began adapting the recipe, that orange chicken gained widespread popularity. The dish was reinvented, incorporating fresh orange juice, zest, and a sticky, tangy sauce that coated the crispy chicken pieces. This modern twist captured the hearts (and taste buds) of diners across the country.

Versatility of Orange Chicken:

One of the remarkable aspects of orange chicken is its versatility. While the classic recipe remains beloved, there are countless ways to put your own spin on this dish. Whether you prefer it spicy, fruity, or even vegetarian, orange chicken can be adapted to suit various palates and dietary preferences.

In the upcoming chapters, we'll explore the different variations and creative twists that you can experiment with. From fusion flavors to healthy adaptations, there's something for everyone to enjoy. Get ready to embark on a culinary adventure that celebrates the vibrant and irresistible allure of orange chicken.

But before we dive into the recipes, let's ensure you have a solid foundation in the essential techniques needed to prepare orange chicken. In the next chapter, we'll master the basics, equipping you with the skills and knowledge to create the perfect orange chicken every time. Get ready to sharpen your culinary prowess as we embark on this delicious journey together.

Chapter 2: Mastering the Basics: Essential Techniques for Preparing Orange Chicken

To create the most delicious orange chicken dishes, it's crucial to master the fundamental techniques that form the foundation of this delectable cuisine. In this chapter, we will explore the essential skills and tips needed to achieve perfection in every bite.

Selecting the Perfect Chicken:

When it comes to orange chicken, choosing the right chicken is paramount. Opt for boneless, skinless chicken thighs for their juicy tenderness, or if you prefer a leaner option, boneless, skinless chicken breast works well too. It's important to ensure that the chicken you select is fresh and of high quality. Look for chicken that is plump, moist, and free from any unpleasant odors or discoloration. You can also consider opting for organic or free-range chicken for enhanced flavor and ethical considerations.

Preparing the Chicken:

Properly preparing the chicken is a crucial step in ensuring optimal flavor and texture. Start by trimming any excess fat from the chicken pieces. This helps to prevent any unwanted greasiness and ensures a cleaner taste.

Additionally, removing fat allows the marinade and sauce to adhere better to the chicken. Next, cut the chicken into bite-sized pieces that are relatively uniform in size. This will help to ensure even cooking and a harmonious balance with the orange sauce. Aim for pieces that are about 1 to 1.5 inches in diameter. Pat the chicken dry with paper towels before proceeding to marination.

Marinating for Maximum Flavor:

Marinating the chicken is a key technique for infusing it with a burst of flavors. Create a marinade using a combination of fresh orange juice, soy sauce, minced garlic, grated ginger, and a touch of sweetness like honey or brown sugar.

The acidity of the orange juice helps to tenderize the chicken while imparting a delightful citrus flavor. The soy sauce adds savory umami notes, while the garlic and ginger contribute aromatic complexity. Combine all the marinade ingredients in a bowl and whisk until well blended.

Place the chicken pieces in a shallow dish or zip-top bag and pour the marinade over them, ensuring that the chicken is fully coated. Massage the marinade into the chicken gently to ensure even distribution. Cover the dish or seal the bag and let the chicken marinate in the refrigerator for at least 30 minutes, allowing the flavors to penetrate the meat.

For an even more pronounced taste, you can marinate the chicken overnight in the refrigerator. The longer marination time allows the flavors to develop further, resulting in a more flavorful and tender orange chicken.

Breading and Frying to Crispy Perfection:
Achieving that coveted crispy exterior is a hallmark of great orange chicken. Start by preparing a light batter for coating the chicken.

Combine cornstarch and all-purpose flour in a bowl, and season it with salt and pepper to taste. The cornstarch helps to create a crispy texture, while the flour adds structure and body to the batter. Whisk the dry ingredients together until well combined. Dip the marinated chicken pieces into the batter, ensuring they are well coated.

Use a fork or tongs to remove the chicken from the marinade, allowing any excess marinade to drip off before coating it in the batter. This will prevent the batter from becoming too thick or clumpy.

Heat oil in a frying pan or wok over medium-high heat. You can use vegetable, canola, or peanut oil for frying, as they have high smoke points and neutral flavors that won't overpower the dish. Carefully add the battered chicken pieces to the hot oil, ensuring not to overcrowd the pan.

Fry the chicken until it turns golden brown and crispy, flipping the pieces occasionally for even cooking.

The high heat helps to seal in the moisture and create that delightful crunch while maintaining the chicken's succulent interior. Once cooked, transfer the fried chicken to a paper towel-lined plate to drain any excess oil.

Creating the Signature Orange Sauce:

The luscious orange sauce is what sets this dish apart. In a saucepan, combine fresh orange juice, orange zest, soy sauce, rice vinegar, sugar, minced garlic, and grated ginger.

Bring the mixture to a simmer over medium heat, stirring occasionally. Allow the sauce to cook until it thickens, becoming glossy and coating the back of a spoon.

This process helps to meld the flavors together and create a harmonious balance of sweet, tangy, and savory notes. The fresh orange juice provides a bright citrusy base, while the orange zest adds a concentrated burst of flavor.

The soy sauce contributes a savory depth, and the rice vinegar brings a subtle tanginess that balances the sweetness of the dish. The garlic and ginger infuse the sauce with aromatic complexity, enhancing the overall flavor profile.

Adjust the sweetness and tanginess of the sauce according to your taste preferences by adding more sugar or vinegar as desired. You can also customize the spiciness level by incorporating red pepper flakes or chili sauce if you prefer a hint of heat.

Balancing Sweet, Tangy, and Savory Flavors:

Achieving the perfect balance of sweet, tangy, and savory flavors is essential in orange chicken.

It's important to taste the sauce as you go and adjust the ingredients accordingly. If you prefer a sweeter sauce, you can add a bit more sugar to the mixture. For a tangier profile, a splash of rice vinegar can do wonders in brightening the flavors.

Remember that the sweetness of the sauce will be balanced by the savory and umami notes of the soy sauce and other ingredients. Strive for a harmonious blend where none of the flavors overpower the others.

Feel free to experiment and fine-tune the flavors to suit your palate, adding more or less of any ingredient until you achieve the desired taste.

Garnishing for Visual Appeal:

Once your orange chicken is ready to be served, don't forget the final touch of garnishing. Sprinkle some toasted sesame seeds over the dish for added texture and nuttiness. You can toast sesame seeds by heating them in a dry pan over medium heat until they turn golden brown and release a fragrant aroma.

Thinly sliced green onions or fresh cilantro can also be used as garnishes, adding a burst of freshness and visual appeal to the vibrant orange chicken. Simply sprinkle them over the dish before serving.

By mastering these essential techniques, you'll be well on your way to creating mouthwatering orange chicken that will leave your taste buds dancing with delight. In the next chapter, we'll dive into the classic orange chicken recipe, ensuring you have a foolproof rendition in your culinary repertoire.

Get ready to savor the iconic flavors that have made orange chicken a beloved dish worldwide.

Chapter 3: Classic Orange Chicken Recipe: A Flavorful Delight

Now that you have mastered the essential techniques for preparing orange chicken, it's time to delve into the classic recipe that has delighted countless taste buds. In this chapter, we will walk you through step-by-step instructions on how to create a mouthwatering orange chicken dish that captures the perfect balance of flavors and textures.

Ingredients:

- 1.5 lbs boneless, skinless chicken thighs or chicken breast
- 1 cup fresh orange juice (about 3-4 oranges)
- Zest of 1 orange
- 1/4 cup soy sauce
- 2 tablespoons rice vinegar
- 3 tablespoons sugar
- 2 cloves garlic, minced
- 1 tablespoon grated ginger

- 1/4 teaspoon red pepper flakes (optional, for added heat)
- 1/4 cup cornstarch
- 1/4 cup all-purpose flour
- Vegetable oil, for frying
- Toasted sesame seeds, for garnish
- Thinly sliced green onions or fresh cilantro, for garnish

Preparing the Chicken:

Start by trimming any excess fat from the chicken thighs or breast. If using chicken thighs, remove any visible skin as well. Cutting against the grain, slice the chicken into bite-sized pieces, ensuring they are relatively uniform in size. This allows for even cooking and consistent texture throughout the dish.

Marinating the Chicken:

In a mixing bowl, combine the fresh orange juice, orange zest, soy sauce, rice vinegar, sugar, minced garlic, grated ginger, and red pepper flakes if desired. Stir well to blend the ingredients and create a flavorful marinade.

The orange juice provides a tangy and citrusy base, while the zest adds a concentrated burst of orange flavor. The soy sauce adds savory depth, and the rice vinegar brings a subtle tanginess.

The sugar balances the flavors and helps to create a slightly sweet glaze. The minced garlic and grated ginger infuse the marinade with aromatic complexity. Add the chicken pieces to the marinade and ensure they are fully coated. Cover the bowl or transfer the mixture to a zip-top bag and refrigerate for at least 30 minutes to allow the flavors to penetrate the meat.

For a more pronounced taste, marinate the chicken overnight.

Preparing the Batter:

In a separate bowl, combine the cornstarch and all-purpose flour. This mixture will form the batter that coats the chicken pieces and gives them a crispy texture. Whisk the dry ingredients together until well combined.

The cornstarch provides a light and crispy coating, while the flour adds structure and body to the batter.

Frying the Chicken:

Heat vegetable oil in a frying pan or wok over medium-high heat. The oil should be about 1 inch deep to ensure the chicken is fully submerged while frying. While the oil is heating, remove the chicken pieces from the marinade, allowing any excess marinade to drip off. This step prevents the batter from becoming too wet or clumpy. Dip each piece into the batter, ensuring it is fully coated. Gently shake off any excess batter.

Carefully place the battered chicken pieces into the hot oil, being cautious not to overcrowd the pan. Fry the chicken until it turns golden brown and crispy, flipping the pieces occasionally for even cooking.

This process usually takes about 4-6 minutes per side. Once cooked, transfer the fried chicken to a paper towel-lined plate to drain any excess oil.

Creating the Orange Sauce:

In a saucepan, combine the remaining marinade (strained to remove any chicken particles) with an additional 1/4 cup of fresh orange juice.

Heat the mixture over medium heat and bring it to a simmer. Allow the sauce to cook and reduce for about 5-7 minutes, until it thickens and develops a glossy consistency.

Stir occasionally to prevent sticking and ensure even heat distribution. The reduction process helps intensify the flavors and create a luscious glaze for the chicken.

Combining the Chicken and Sauce:

Once the sauce has thickened, add the fried chicken pieces to the saucepan. Gently toss the chicken in the sauce until each piece is fully coated.

Continue to cook for an additional 1-2 minutes, allowing the flavors to meld together. This step ensures that every bite of chicken is infused with the tangy and sweet orange sauce.

Serving the Orange Chicken:

Transfer the orange chicken to a serving platter. Garnish with toasted sesame seeds, thinly sliced green onions, or fresh cilantro for an extra pop of flavor and visual appeal. The garnishes add freshness and complement the vibrant orange color of the dish. They also provide a pleasant textural contrast.

Serve the orange chicken hot with steamed rice or noodles for a complete and satisfying meal.

By following these detailed steps, you'll be able to recreate the classic orange chicken recipe with confidence and finesse. Feel free to experiment with additional ingredients or modifications to suit your personal preferences. In the next chapter, we will explore variations of orange chicken that incorporate unique flavors and ingredients, allowing you to expand your culinary repertoire and impress your guests with exciting twists on this beloved dish. Get ready to embark on a flavor adventure!

Chapter 4: Variations of Orange Chicken: Exploring New Flavors

While the classic orange chicken recipe is undeniably delicious, there's always room to experiment and add your own personal touch to the dish. In this chapter, we will explore various flavor variations of orange chicken that will elevate your culinary repertoire and introduce exciting new tastes. From spicy and tangy to sweet and savory, these variations will ignite your taste buds and leave you craving for more.

Spicy Orange Chicken:

For those who enjoy a bit of heat, the spicy orange chicken variation will add a fiery kick to your meal. To create this version, you can increase the amount of red pepper flakes in the marinade and sauce. Alternatively, you can add a tablespoon or two of chili sauce, such as Sriracha or sambal oelek, to the mix. Adjust the amount of spice according to your preference.

The spicy element will contrast with the tangy and sweet orange flavors, creating a tantalizing combination. Serve it with steamed jasmine rice to balance the heat.

Honey Orange Chicken:

If you have a penchant for sweetness, the honey orange chicken variation is a delightful option. To make this version, substitute a portion of the sugar in the marinade and sauce with honey. The natural sweetness of honey adds a rich and luxurious flavor to the dish.

It caramelizes beautifully, creating a glossy glaze that coats the chicken. The combination of honey and orange creates a harmonious balance of flavors. Garnish with toasted sesame seeds and thinly sliced green onions for added texture and freshness.

Ginger Orange Chicken:

To infuse your orange chicken with a warm and aromatic twist, the ginger orange chicken variation is perfect. Increase the amount of grated ginger in the marinade and sauce to intensify its flavor. Ginger adds a subtle spiciness and earthy note that complements the bright flavors of orange.

It also provides a refreshing and cleansing element to the dish. Consider adding some sautéed or pickled ginger as a garnish to enhance the ginger profile even further.

Garlic Orange Chicken:

For garlic enthusiasts, the garlic orange chicken variation will satisfy your cravings. Increase the amount of minced garlic in the marinade and sauce to intensify its aroma and taste. Garlic adds a savory and robust umami flavor that pairs beautifully with the tangy sweetness of orange.

The combination creates a bold and satisfying dish. Serve it with steamed Bok choy or broccoli to add a fresh and crunchy element.

Teriyaki Orange Chicken:

Merge two beloved Asian flavors by combining orange chicken with teriyaki sauce. Prepare the classic orange chicken as per the recipe but add a touch of teriyaki sauce to the marinade and sauce mixture.

Teriyaki sauce brings a savory and slightly sweet profile that complements the tanginess of the orange. It adds depth and richness to the dish. Serve it over a bed of stir-fried vegetables or alongside steamed jasmine rice for a complete meal.

Sesame Orange Chicken:

Take your orange chicken to a nutty and toasty level with the sesame orange chicken variation. Incorporate sesame seeds into the recipe by either adding them to the batter or sprinkling them over the finished dish as a garnish.

Toasted sesame seeds add a delightful crunch and nutty flavor to the chicken, enhancing its overall texture. You can also drizzle some toasted sesame oil over the chicken for an extra hint of nuttiness.

Citrus Orange Chicken:

Expand the citrus flavor profile of your orange chicken by incorporating other citrus fruits. Experiment with adding lemon or lime juice and zest to the marinade and sauce. The tangy and bright flavors of these citrus fruits will complement the orange and add a refreshing twist to the dish.

The combination of multiple citrus flavors creates a complex and vibrant taste experience. Serve it with a side of citrus-infused couscous or quinoa for a complete citrusy experience.

Remember, these variations are just the beginning. Feel free to get creative and combine different flavors and ingredients to make the orange chicken your own. Whether you prefer it spicy, sweet, or with a unique twist, the possibilities are endless. In the next chapter, we will explore side dishes and accompaniments that pair perfectly with orange chicken, enhancing the overall dining experience. Get ready to elevate your meal to new heights!

Chapter 5: Side Dishes and Accompaniments: Enhancing the Orange Chicken Experience

No great meal is complete without carefully selected side dishes and accompaniments that complement the star of the show—the orange chicken. In this chapter, we will explore a range of options that will elevate your dining experience, offering a perfect balance of flavors, textures, and colors. From refreshing salads to hearty grains, these side dishes will enhance the overall enjoyment of your orange chicken feast.

Steamed Jasmine Rice:

A classic and versatile option steamed jasmine rice is a staple that pairs wonderfully with orange chicken. To prepare it, rinse the rice thoroughly and then cook it using the absorption method, following the package instructions.

The light and fragrant jasmine rice acts as a neutral canvas, allowing the flavors of the orange chicken to shine. The grains are fluffy and delicately scented, providing a subtle aromatic undertone to the dish. Serve it on the side or create a bed of rice for the orange chicken to rest upon, allowing the flavors to mingle.

Chow Mein Noodles:

For those craving a heartier side dish, chow Mein noodles are an excellent choice. These Chinese stir-fried noodles offer a delightful chewiness and a savory undertone that complements the orange chicken perfectly.

To prepare chow Mein noodles, boil them until al dente, then stir-fry them with a medley of crisp vegetables such as bell peppers, carrots, bean sprouts, and scallions.

The combination of textures—from the tender noodles to the crunchy vegetables—adds a satisfying contrast to the tender orange chicken. Drizzle some soy sauce or sesame oil over the noodles for an extra layer of flavor.

Stir-Fried Vegetables:

A colorful medley of stir-fried vegetables is a refreshing addition to the orange chicken dish. Heat a wok or skillet over high heat and add a drizzle of oil. Sauté a combination of bell peppers (red, green, and yellow), snap peas, broccoli florets, carrots, and baby corn until they are tender-crisp.

The vibrant colors and crisp textures of the stir-fried vegetables provide a pleasant contrast to the tender chicken.

Season the vegetables with a light soy sauce or a touch of garlic for added depth of flavor. The freshness and crunchiness of the stir-fried vegetables enhance the overall dining experience.

Asian Slaw:

Add a refreshing and crunchy element to your orange chicken meal with an Asian-inspired slaw. Shred cabbage, carrots, and radishes into thin strips and toss them together in a mixing bowl. For the dressing, whisk together rice vinegar, soy sauce, sesame oil, a touch of honey or sugar, and a sprinkle of salt.

The tangy and slightly sweet flavors of the slaw beautifully balance the richness of the orange chicken.

Mix the dressing with the shredded vegetables and let the flavors meld for a few minutes before serving. Sprinkle some toasted sesame seeds or chopped cilantro on top for extra visual appeal and a burst of flavor.

Steamed Bok Choy:

For a simple yet flavorful side, steamed Bok choy is an excellent choice. Bok choy, with its tender-crisp texture and mild, slightly bitter taste, provides a refreshing counterpoint to the bold flavors of the orange chicken.

To prepare steamed Bok choy, trim off the bottom ends of the stalks and cut the leaves into manageable pieces. Place the Bok choy in a steamer basket over boiling water and steam for a few minutes until it becomes tender but still retains its vibrant green color.

Drizzle with a touch of soy sauce or sesame oil for added flavor. The lightness and simplicity of steamed Bok choy make it a versatile and healthy accompaniment to the orange chicken.

Fried Rice:

Transform leftover steamed rice into a delicious and satisfying side dish by preparing fried rice. This classic Chinese dish is a great way to repurpose cooked rice and add a flavorful twist to your meal.

Start by heating a wok or large skillet over medium-high heat and adding a drizzle of oil. Add diced vegetables such as carrots, peas, onions, and any other preferred vegetables, and stir-fry until they become tender. Push the vegetables to the side of the wok and crack a few eggs into the empty space, scrambling them until cooked.

Add the cooked rice to the wok along with soy sauce, minced garlic, grated ginger, and a pinch of salt. Stir-fry everything together until well combined and heated through. The combination of flavors in the fried rice pairs beautifully with the orange chicken, creating a balanced and complete meal.

Quinoa Salad:

For a nutritious and protein-rich option, a quinoa salad with fresh herbs and vegetables is a great choice. Rinse the quinoa thoroughly and cook it according to the package instructions.

Once cooked, let it cool to room temperature. In a large mixing bowl, combine the cooked quinoa with diced cucumbers, cherry tomatoes, red onions, chopped cilantro, and any other preferred vegetables.

For the dressing, whisk together fresh lime juice, extra-virgin olive oil, a touch of honey or agave nectar, salt, and pepper. Drizzle the dressing over the salad and toss to coat all the ingredients.

The light and zesty flavors of the quinoa salad provide a refreshing contrast to the richness of the orange chicken. The salad can be served chilled or at room temperature.

Steamed Edamame:

A simple and healthy side dish, steamed edamame is a great option to accompany orange chicken. Edamame are young soybeans that are harvested before they fully mature.

To prepare them, simply boil them in salted water for a few minutes until they become tender. Drain the edamame and sprinkle them with a pinch of sea salt.

The vibrant green pods can be served in a bowl alongside the orange chicken, allowing everyone to enjoy the satisfying ritual of popping the beans out of the pods and savoring their mildly nutty flavor.

Edamame is not only delicious but also packed with protein and fiber, adding a nutritious element to your meal.

Remember, the choice of side dishes and accompaniments ultimately depends on your personal preferences and the overall theme of your meal. Feel free to mix and match or experiment with different combinations to find your perfect pairing. In the next chapter, we will dive into the realm of desserts and treats inspired by the flavors of orange chicken. Get ready for a sweet and satisfying conclusion to your culinary journey!

Chapter 6: Sweet Endings: Desserts Inspired by Orange Chicken

After savoring the delectable flavors of orange chicken, it's time to indulge in a sweet ending to your culinary journey. In this chapter, we will explore desserts and treats that draw inspiration from the vibrant citrus notes and delightful spices found in orange chicken. These mouthwatering creations will satisfy your sweet tooth and leave you with a memorable finale to your orange chicken feast.

Orange-infused Pound Cake:

Delve into the realm of citrusy sweetness with an orange-infused pound cake. The combination of buttery richness and zesty orange flavor creates a harmonious balance that will captivate your taste buds. Begin by preparing a classic pound cake batter with flour, sugar, butter, eggs, and a touch of vanilla extract. To infuse the cake with orange goodness, grate the zest of fresh oranges and add it to the batter along with a splash of freshly squeezed orange juice.

The aroma that fills your kitchen as the cake bakes is irresistible. Once golden and fragrant, let the cake cool before drizzling it with a simple glaze made from powdered sugar and orange juice. The result is a moist and tender pound cake with a burst of citrus flavor that pairs beautifully with a cup of tea or coffee.

Citrus Fruit Salad:

For a refreshing and vibrant dessert, prepare a citrus fruit salad that showcases the bright and tangy flavors of oranges, grapefruits, tangerines, and pomelos. Peel and segment the fruits, removing any pith and seeds.

Arrange the citrus segments in a bowl, allowing their jewel-like colors to create an enticing display. To enhance the natural sweetness and add a touch of freshness, garnish the salad with a sprinkle of finely chopped mint leaves.

The combination of juicy citrus fruits and the aromatic hint of mint provides a light and invigorating dessert option that complements the flavors of orange chicken. For an extra touch, drizzle a honey-lime dressing over the fruit salad, adding a delightful tanginess to the ensemble.

Ginger Orange Sorbet:

Cool down and tantalize your taste buds with a ginger orange sorbet that blends the zesty tang of oranges with the warming spice of ginger.

Start by combining freshly squeezed orange juice, grated ginger, sugar, and water in a saucepan. Allow the mixture to simmer until the sugar dissolves and the flavors meld together.

Once cooled, strain the mixture to remove the ginger pieces. Transfer the liquid to an ice cream maker and churn according to the manufacturer's instructions until it reaches a smooth and creamy consistency.

The resulting sorbet is a delightful balance of citrusy sweetness with a hint of ginger heat. Each spoonful offers a refreshing burst of flavor that cools and invigorates the palate, providing a perfect contrast to the savory notes of the orange chicken.

Orange Cream Puffs:

Indulge in a delectable combination of airy cream puffs filled with a luscious, orange-infused cream.

The light and delicate choux pastry shells provide a delightful contrast to the creamy and citrusy filling. Begin by preparing the choux pastry dough, which involves heating water, butter, and a pinch of salt in a saucepan until the butter melts. Stir in flour and continue cooking and stirring until the dough forms a ball.

Transfer the dough to a mixing bowl and let it cool slightly. Gradually add eggs, one at a time, beating well after each addition, until the dough becomes smooth and glossy. Drop spoonful of the dough onto a baking sheet and bake until puffed and golden. As the cream puffs cool, prepare the orange-infused cream filling.

Whip heavy cream with powdered sugar and a splash of orange extract until stiff peaks form. Cut the cooled cream puffs in half and generously fill them with the orange cream. To add a touch of elegance, dust the tops of the cream puffs with powdered sugar. With each bite, you'll experience the delicate pastry, velvety cream, and vibrant citrus flavor, creating a heavenly dessert experience.

Orange Gingerbread Cookies:

Add a twist to a beloved classic by infusing gingerbread cookies with the flavors of orange.

These cookies offer a delightful combination of warm spices and bright citrus zest. Begin by preparing a gingerbread cookie dough using flour, brown sugar, molasses, ground ginger, cinnamon, nutmeg, cloves, baking soda, and a pinch of salt.

To infuse the dough with a burst of orange, add freshly grated orange zest and a dash of orange juice. Roll out the dough and cut it into festive shapes using cookie cutters. As the cookies bake, your kitchen will be filled with the irresistible aroma of gingerbread and orange.

Once golden and slightly crisp, remove the cookies from the oven and let them cool before enjoying. These cookies can be enjoyed on their own, or you can get creative and decorate them with a drizzle of orange-flavored glaze or colorful icing for a festive touch.

Each bite delivers a perfect balance of spicy warmth and citrus brightness, making these cookies a delightful treat for any occasion.

Remember, these desserts are inspired by the flavors of orange chicken and offer a delightful conclusion to your culinary adventure. They showcase the versatility of oranges and their ability to transform ordinary desserts into extraordinary delights. As you savor these sweet creations, reflect on the diverse and delicious journey you've embarked upon with the orange chicken cookbook.

Chapter 7: Mastering Orange Chicken Variations

Now that you have mastered the art of preparing classic orange chicken and discovered a variety of side dishes and desserts to accompany it, it's time to explore the world of orange chicken variations. In this chapter, we will delve into creative twists and unique flavor profiles that will take your orange chicken game to the next level. Get ready to unleash your culinary creativity and surprise your taste buds with these exciting variations.

Spicy Orange Chicken:

Ingredients:

- 1-pound boneless, skinless chicken breasts, cut into bite-sized pieces
- 2 tablespoons vegetable oil
- 2 cloves garlic, minced
- 1 teaspoon fresh ginger, grated
- 1/4 teaspoon red pepper flakes (adjust to taste)
- 1/2 cup orange juice
- 2 tablespoons soy sauce
- 2 tablespoons honey
- 1 tablespoon rice vinegar
- 1 teaspoon cornstarch
- Salt and pepper, to taste
- Green onions, sliced (for garnish)
- Sesame seeds (for garnish)

Instructions:

1. In a small bowl, whisk together the orange juice, soy sauce,

honey, rice vinegar, and cornstarch. Set aside.

2. Heat the vegetable oil in a large skillet or wok over medium-high heat. Add the minced garlic, grated ginger, and red pepper flakes. Cook for about 30 seconds until fragrant.

3. Add the chicken pieces to the skillet and cook until browned and cooked through, about 4-5 minutes.

4. Pour the prepared orange sauce over the chicken in the skillet. Stir well to coat the chicken evenly. Cook for another 2-3 minutes until the sauce thickens and coats the chicken.

5. Season with salt and pepper to taste. Remove from heat.

6. Serve the spicy orange chicken over steamed rice or noodles. Garnish with sliced green onions and sesame seeds for added flavor and presentation.

Sesame Orange Chicken:
Ingredients:

- 1-pound boneless, skinless chicken thighs, cut into bite-sized pieces
- 2 tablespoons vegetable oil
- 2 cloves garlic, minced
- 1 teaspoon fresh ginger, grated
- 1/2 cup orange juice
- 2 tablespoons soy sauce
- 2 tablespoons honey
- 1 tablespoon sesame oil
- 1 tablespoon cornstarch
- 2 tablespoons sesame seeds, toasted
- Green onions, sliced (for garnish)

Instructions:

1. In a small bowl, whisk together the orange juice, soy sauce, honey, sesame oil, and cornstarch. Set aside.
2. Heat the vegetable oil in a large skillet or wok over medium-high heat. Add the minced garlic and grated ginger. Cook for about 30 seconds until fragrant.
3. Add the chicken pieces to the skillet and cook until browned and cooked through, about 4-5 minutes.
4. Pour the prepared orange sauce over the chicken in the skillet. Stir well to coat the chicken evenly. Cook for another 2-3 minutes until the sauce thickens and coats the chicken.
5. Sprinkle the toasted sesame seeds over the chicken and toss to combine.
6. Remove from heat and garnish with sliced green onions.
7. Serve the sesame orange chicken over steamed rice or noodles. Enjoy the nutty and aromatic flavors!

Orange Ginger Chicken:
Ingredients:

- 1-pound boneless, skinless chicken breasts, cut into bite-sized pieces
- 2 tablespoons vegetable oil
- 2 cloves garlic, minced
- 1 teaspoon fresh ginger, grated
- 1/4 cup orange juice
- 2 tablespoons soy sauce
- 2 tablespoons honey
- 1 tablespoon rice vinegar
- 1 teaspoon cornstarch
- 1 tablespoon sesame oil
- Green onions, sliced (for garnish)

Instructions:

1. In a small bowl, whisk together the orange juice, soy sauce, honey, rice vinegar, cornstarch, and sesame oil. Set aside.
2. Heat the vegetable oil in a large skillet or wok over medium-high heat. Add the minced garlic and grated ginger. Cook for about 30 seconds until fragrant.
3. Add the chicken pieces to the skillet and cook until browned and cooked through, about 4-5 minutes.
4. Pour the prepared orange sauce over the chicken in the skillet. Stir well to coat the chicken evenly. Cook for another 2-3 minutes until the sauce thickens and coats the chicken.
5. Remove from heat and garnish with sliced green onions.
6. Serve the orange ginger chicken over steamed rice or noodles. Enjoy the zingy and aromatic flavors!

Honey Orange Chicken:
Ingredients:

- 1-pound boneless, skinless chicken thighs, cut into bite-sized pieces
- 2 tablespoons vegetable oil
- 2 cloves garlic, minced
- 1 teaspoon fresh ginger, grated
- 1/2 cup orange juice
- 2 tablespoons soy sauce
- 2 tablespoons honey
- 1 tablespoon rice vinegar
- 1 teaspoon cornstarch
- Green onions, sliced (for garnish)
- Orange slices (for garnish)

Instructions:

1. In a small bowl, whisk together the orange juice, soy sauce, honey, rice vinegar, and cornstarch. Set it aside.
2. Heat the vegetable oil in a large skillet or wok over medium-high heat. Add the minced garlic and grated ginger. Cook for about 30 seconds until fragrant.
3. Add the chicken pieces to the skillet and cook until browned and cooked through, about 4-5 minutes.
4. Pour the prepared orange sauce over the chicken in the skillet. Stir well to coat the chicken evenly. Cook for another 2-3 minutes until the sauce thickens and coats the chicken.
5. Remove from heat and garnish with sliced green onions and orange slices.
6. Serve the honey orange chicken over steamed rice or noodles. Enjoy the natural sweetness and luscious glaze!

Orange Teriyaki Chicken:
Ingredients:

- 1-pound boneless, skinless chicken breasts, cut into bite-sized pieces
- 2 tablespoons vegetable oil
- 2 cloves garlic, minced
- 1 teaspoon fresh ginger, grated
- 1/2 cup orange juice
- 2 tablespoons soy sauce
- 2 tablespoons honey
- 2 tablespoons mirin (sweet rice wine)
- 1 tablespoon rice vinegar
- 1 teaspoon cornstarch
- Sesame seeds (for garnish)
- Sliced green onions (for garnish)

Instructions:

1. In a small bowl, whisk together the orange juice, soy sauce, honey, mirin, rice vinegar, and cornstarch. Set aside.
2. Heat the vegetable oil in a large skillet or wok over medium-high heat. Add the minced garlic and grated ginger. Cook for about 30 seconds until fragrant.
3. Add the chicken pieces to the skillet and cook until browned and cooked through, about 4-5 minutes.
4. Pour the prepared orange teriyaki sauce over the chicken in the skillet. Stir well to coat the chicken evenly. Cook for another 2-3 minutes until the sauce thickens and coats the chicken.
5. Remove from heat and garnish with sesame seeds and sliced green onions.
6. Serve the orange teriyaki chicken over steamed rice or noodles. Enjoy the fusion of tangy and savory flavors!

By experimenting with these tantalizing orange chicken variations, you'll expand your culinary repertoire and discover new flavor combinations that will impress your family and friends. Have fun exploring the possibilities and enjoy the delicious journey of mastering orange chicken in its many delightful forms.

Chapter 8: Orange Chicken Fusion: Global Inspirations

In this chapter, we will embark on a culinary journey around the world, exploring how different cultures incorporate the flavors of orange chicken into their cuisines. Prepare to be inspired by the diverse and mouthwatering dishes that combine the essence of orange chicken with unique ingredients and cooking techniques. Let's dive into the global fusion of orange chicken!

Orange Chicken Stir-Fry with Bok Choy (Chinese-Inspired):
Ingredients:

- 1-pound boneless, skinless chicken thighs, cut into strips
- 2 tablespoons vegetable oil
- 2 cloves garlic, minced
- 1 teaspoon fresh ginger, grated
- 1/4 cup orange juice
- 2 tablespoons soy sauce
- 2 tablespoons hoisin sauce
- 1 tablespoon honey
- 1 tablespoon cornstarch
- 1 bunch Bok choy, chopped
- Sesame seeds (for garnish)
- Cooked rice (for serving)

Instructions:

1. Heat the vegetable oil in a large skillet or wok over medium-high heat. Add the minced garlic and grated ginger. Cook for about 30 seconds until fragrant.
2. Add the chicken strips to the skillet and cook until browned and cooked through, about 5-6 minutes.
3. In a small bowl, whisk together the orange juice, soy sauce, hoisin sauce, honey, and cornstarch. Pour the sauce mixture over the chicken in the skillet.
4. Add the chopped Bok choy to the skillet and stir-fry for 2-3 minutes until it starts to wilt.
5. Continue cooking for another 2-3 minutes until the sauce thickens and coats the chicken and Bok choy.
6. Remove from heat and garnish with sesame seeds.
7. Serve the orange chicken stir-fry with Bok choy over cooked rice. Enjoy the combination of tender chicken, vibrant Bok choy, and tangy orange flavors.

Orange Glazed Salmon (Asian Fusion):
Ingredients:

- 4 salmon fillets
- 1/4 cup orange juice
- 2 tablespoons soy sauce
- 2 tablespoons honey
- 1 tablespoon rice vinegar
- 1 teaspoon grated orange zest
- 2 cloves garlic, minced
- 1 teaspoon fresh ginger, grated
- 1 tablespoon vegetable oil
- Green onions, sliced (for garnish)
- Sesame seeds (for garnish)

Instructions:

1. In a small bowl, whisk together the orange juice, soy sauce, honey, rice vinegar, orange zest, minced garlic, and grated ginger to create the glaze.
2. Heat the vegetable oil in a skillet over medium-high heat. Place the salmon fillets in the skillet, skin-side down, and cook for about 4-5 minutes until browned.
3. Flip the salmon fillets and pour the glaze over the top. Continue cooking for another 3-4 minutes until the salmon is cooked through and the glaze has thickened.
4. Remove from heat and garnish with sliced green onions and sesame seeds.
5. Serve the orange-glazed salmon with steamed rice or roasted vegetables. Enjoy the succulent salmon infused with the tangy and sweet flavors of orange.

Orange Chicken Tacos (Mexican Fusion):

Ingredients:

- 1-pound boneless, skinless chicken breasts, thinly sliced
- 2 tablespoons vegetable oil
- 2 cloves garlic, minced
- 1 teaspoon ground cumin
- 1 teaspoon chili powder
- 1/2 teaspoon paprika
- 1/4 teaspoon cayenne pepper (adjust to taste)
- 1/4 cup orange juice
- 1 tablespoon lime juice
- Salt and pepper, to taste
- Tortillas (corn or flour)
- Shredded lettuce
- Diced tomatoes
- Avocado slices
- Fresh cilantro (for garnish)

Instructions:

1. Heat the vegetable oil in a skillet over medium heat. Add the minced garlic and sauté for about 1 minute until fragrant.
2. Add the chicken slices to the skillet and season with ground cumin, chili powder, paprika, cayenne pepper, salt, and pepper. Cook for about 5-6 minutes until the chicken is cooked through and nicely browned.
3. Pour the orange juice and lime juice over the chicken in the skillet. Stir well to coat the chicken with the citrus flavors. Cook for another 2-3 minutes to allow the flavors to meld.
4. Warm the tortillas according to the package instructions.
5. Fill each tortilla with a portion of the orange chicken, shredded lettuce, diced tomatoes, avocado slices, and fresh cilantro.
6. Serve the orange chicken tacos as a delightful fusion of Mexican

and Asian flavors. Enjoy the vibrant and zesty combination!

Orange Chicken Curry (Indian Fusion):
Ingredients:

- 1-pound boneless, skinless chicken thighs, cut into bite-sized pieces
- 2 tablespoons vegetable oil
- 1 onion, finely chopped
- 2 cloves garlic, minced
- 1 teaspoon fresh ginger, grated
- 2 teaspoons curry powder
- 1 teaspoon ground cumin
- 1/2 teaspoon turmeric powder
- 1/4 teaspoon cayenne pepper (adjust to taste)
- 1 cup tomato puree
- 1/2 cup orange juice
- 1/2 cup coconut milk
- Salt, to taste
- Fresh cilantro (for garnish)
- Cooked basmati rice or naan bread (for serving)

Instructions:

1. Heat the vegetable oil in a large skillet or pot over medium heat. Add the chopped onion and sauté until translucent.
2. Add the minced garlic and grated ginger to the skillet. Cook for about 1 minute until fragrant.
3. Add the chicken pieces to the skillet and cook until browned on all sides, about 5-6 minutes.
4. In a small bowl, combine the curry powder, ground cumin, turmeric powder, and cayenne pepper. Sprinkle the spice mixture over the chicken in the skillet and stir well to coat.
5. Pour in the tomato puree and orange juice. Stir to combine all the ingredients.

6. Reduce the heat to low, cover the skillet or pot, and let the curry simmer for about 20-25 minutes, stirring occasionally.
7. Stir in the coconut milk and season with salt to taste. Cook for another 5 minutes to heat the coconut milk through.
8. Remove from heat and garnish with fresh cilantro.
9. Serve the aromatic orange chicken curry with basmati rice or naan bread for a delightful fusion of Indian and citrus flavors.

By incorporating global influences into your orange chicken dishes, you can create exciting and unique flavor combinations that will transport your taste buds to different parts of the world. Explore the fusion of cuisines and let your culinary creativity shine with these mouthwatering recipes. Enjoy the diverse and captivating flavors of orange chicken fusion!

Chapter 9: Light and Healthy Orange Chicken Options

In this chapter, we'll explore lighter and healthier variations of orange chicken that are perfect for those seeking nutritious options without compromising on flavor. These recipes focus on using lean proteins, fresh ingredients, and smart cooking techniques to create delicious and guilt-free orange chicken dishes. Let's dive into the world of light and healthy orange chicken!

Orange Grilled Chicken Skewers:

Ingredients:

- 1-pound boneless, skinless chicken breasts, cut into chunks
- 1/4 cup orange juice
- 2 tablespoons low-sodium soy sauce
- 1 tablespoon honey
- 1 tablespoon olive oil
- 2 cloves garlic, minced
- 1 teaspoon grated orange zest
- Salt and pepper, to taste
- Skewers (soaked in water for 30 minutes)

Instructions:

1. In a bowl, whisk together the orange juice, soy sauce, honey, olive oil, minced garlic, orange zest, salt, and pepper to create the marinade.
2. Add the chicken chunks to the marinade, ensuring they are well coated. Let it marinate in the refrigerator for at least 30 minutes or up to 2 hours.
3. Preheat the grill to medium-high heat.
4. Thread the marinated chicken chunks onto the soaked skewers.

5. Place the chicken skewers on the preheated grill and cook for about 6-8 minutes per side until the chicken is cooked through and slightly charred.

6. Remove from the grill and let them rest for a few minutes before serving.

7. Serve the orange grilled chicken skewers as a light and protein-packed option, perfect for summer barbecues or as a flavorful addition to salads.

Orange Quinoa Salad with Grilled Shrimp:
Ingredients:

- 1 cup quinoa, cooked according to package instructions and cooled
- 1-pound large shrimp, peeled and deveined
- 1/4 cup orange juice
- 2 tablespoons olive oil
- 1 tablespoon honey
- 1 teaspoon Dijon mustard
- 1/2 teaspoon grated orange zest
- Salt and pepper, to taste
- Mixed salad greens
- Cherry tomatoes, halved
- Sliced cucumbers
- Sliced almonds (for garnish)
- Fresh cilantro (for garnish)

Instructions:

1. In a small bowl, whisk together the orange juice, olive oil, honey, Dijon mustard, orange zest, salt, and pepper to create the dressing.
2. Preheat the grill to medium-high heat.
3. Toss the shrimp in the prepared dressing, making sure they are well coated. Let them marinate for about 15 minutes.
4. Grill the marinated shrimp for 2-3 minutes per side until they are pink and cooked through.
5. In a large salad bowl, combine the cooked quinoa, mixed salad greens, cherry tomatoes, and sliced cucumbers.
6. Drizzle the remaining dressing over the salad and toss to combine.

7. Top the salad with the grilled shrimp.
8. Garnish with sliced almonds and fresh cilantro.
9. Serve the orange quinoa salad with grilled shrimp as a refreshing and nutritious option, packed with protein, whole grains, and vibrant flavors.

Baked Orange Chicken Tenders:
Ingredients:

- 1 pound chicken tenders
- 1/2 cup orange juice
- 2 tablespoons low-sodium soy sauce
- 1 tablespoon honey
- 1 teaspoon grated orange zest
- 1/2 cup whole wheat breadcrumbs
- 1/4 cup grated Parmesan cheese
- 1/2 teaspoon paprika
- Salt and pepper, to taste
- Cooking spray

Instructions:

1. Preheat the oven to 425°F (220°C). Line a baking sheet with parchment paper and lightly coat it with cooking spray.
2. In a shallow dish, whisk together the orange juice, soy sauce, honey, and grated orange zest.
3. In another shallow dish, combine the whole wheat breadcrumbs, grated Parmesan cheese, paprika, salt, and pepper.
4. Dip each chicken tender into the orange juice mixture, allowing any excess to drip off, then coat it in the breadcrumb mixture, pressing gently to adhere.
5. Place the coated chicken tenders on the prepared baking sheet.
6. Lightly spray the top of the chicken tenders with cooking spray.
7. Bake for about 15-18 minutes until the chicken is cooked through and the coating is golden and crispy.
8. Remove from the oven and let them cool for a few minutes before serving.
9. Serve the baked orange chicken tenders as a healthier alternative to traditional fried chicken tenders, paired with a

side of steamed vegetables or a salad.

These light and healthy orange chicken options allow you to enjoy the flavors you love while maintaining a balanced and nutritious diet. Embrace these recipes as guilt-free alternatives that are equally delicious and satisfying. Indulge in the goodness of orange chicken without compromising on your health goals!

Chapter 10: Orange Chicken for Special Occasions

In this chapter, we'll explore orange chicken recipes that are perfect for special occasions and gatherings. Whether you're hosting a dinner party, celebrating a holiday, or simply want to elevate your everyday meal, these recipes will impress your guests and create memorable dining experiences. Get ready to indulge in the decadence of orange chicken for those extra special moments!

Orange Glazed Cornish Hens:

Ingredients:

- 2 Cornish hens
- 1 cup orange juice
- 1/2 cup brown sugar
- 1/4 cup soy sauce
- 2 tablespoons orange marmalade
- 2 cloves garlic, minced
- 1 teaspoon grated orange zest
- 1/2 teaspoon dried thyme
- Salt and pepper, to taste
- Fresh parsley (for garnish)

Instructions:

1. Preheat the oven to 375°F (190°C).
2. In a saucepan, combine the orange juice, brown sugar, soy sauce, orange marmalade, minced garlic, grated orange zest, dried thyme, salt, and pepper. Bring the mixture to a simmer over medium heat and cook for 5 minutes until slightly thickened.
3. Season the Cornish hens with salt and pepper, inside and out.
4. Place the hens in a roasting pan and brush them generously with

the prepared orange glaze.

5. Roast the hens in the preheated oven for about 50-60 minutes, basting with the glaze every 15 minutes, until the internal temperature reaches 165°F (74°C) and the skin is golden and crispy.

6. Remove the hens from the oven and let them rest for a few minutes before serving.

7. Garnish with fresh parsley for an elegant presentation.

8. Serve the orange glazed Cornish hens as a centerpiece dish for a special occasion, accompanied by roasted vegetables or your favorite side dishes.

Orange Chicken Roulade:
Ingredients:

- 4 boneless, skinless chicken breasts
- Salt and pepper, to taste
- 4 slices Swiss cheese
- 8 slices prosciutto
- 1 cup fresh spinach leaves
- 1/4 cup orange marmalade
- 1/4 cup breadcrumbs
- 1 tablespoon olive oil
- Fresh thyme (for garnish)

Instructions:

1. Preheat the oven to 375°F (190°C).
2. Butterfly the chicken breasts by slicing them horizontally, without cutting all the way through, and then open them like a book.
3. Pound the chicken breasts to an even thickness and season with salt and pepper.
4. Lay a slice of Swiss cheese on each chicken breast, followed by 2 slices of prosciutto and a handful of fresh spinach leaves.
5. Roll up each chicken breast tightly and secure with toothpicks.
6. Place the rolled chicken breasts on a baking sheet lined with parchment paper.
7. Brush the tops of the chicken roulades with orange marmalade and sprinkle breadcrumbs over them.
8. Drizzle olive oil over the top to help brown the breadcrumbs.
9. Bake in the preheated oven for 25-30 minutes until the chicken is cooked through and the breadcrumbs are golden.
10. Remove from the oven and let them rest for a few minutes before removing the toothpicks.

11. Garnish with fresh thyme for a touch of freshness.

12. Serve the orange chicken roulade as an impressive and sophisticated dish for a dinner party, accompanied by a side of roasted potatoes or a colorful salad.

Orange Chicken Stuffed Bell Peppers:
Ingredients:

- 4 bell peppers (assorted colors)
- 1 pound ground chicken
- 1/2 cup cooked white rice
- 1/4 cup diced onion
- 1/4 cup diced carrots
- 1/4 cup diced celery
- 1/4 cup orange juice
- 2 tablespoons soy sauce
- 1 tablespoon honey
- 1 teaspoon grated orange zest
- 1/2 teaspoon ground ginger
- 1/2 teaspoon garlic powder
- Salt and pepper, to taste
- Grated Parmesan cheese (for topping)
- Chopped fresh parsley (for garnish)

Instructions:

1. Preheat the oven to 375°F (190°C).
2. Cut off the tops of the bell peppers and remove the seeds and membranes.
3. In a skillet, cook the ground chicken over medium heat until browned and cooked through. Drain any excess fat.
4. Add the diced onion, carrots, and celery to the skillet and cook for a few minutes until the vegetables are slightly softened.
5. In a small bowl, whisk together the orange juice, soy sauce, honey, grated orange zest, ground ginger, garlic powder, salt, and pepper. Pour the mixture into the skillet and stir to combine.
6. Add the cooked white rice to the skillet and mix well until all

the ingredients are evenly incorporated.

7. Stuff the bell peppers with the chicken and rice mixture, pressing it down gently.
8. Place the stuffed bell peppers in a baking dish and cover with foil.
9. Bake in the preheated oven for 25-30 minutes until the peppers are tender.
10. Remove the foil, sprinkle grated Parmesan cheese over the top of each pepper, and return to the oven for an additional 5 minutes until the cheese is melted and lightly golden.
11. Remove from the oven and let them cool for a few minutes before serving.
12. Garnish with chopped fresh parsley for a pop of color.
13. Serve the orange chicken stuffed bell peppers as an elegant and flavorful dish that will impress your guests at any special occasion.

These special occasion orange chicken recipes are designed to elevate your dining experience and create unforgettable moments. From roasted Cornish hens to elegant chicken roulades and stuffed bell peppers, these dishes are sure to leave a lasting impression. Embrace the indulgence and celebrate in style with these extraordinary orange chicken creations!

Chapter 11: International Flavors of Orange Chicken

In this chapter, we'll take a culinary journey around the world to discover how different cultures incorporate the vibrant flavors of orange chicken into their cuisines. From Asian-inspired dishes to Mediterranean delights, these recipes will introduce you to unique and exciting variations of orange chicken that will expand your palate and satisfy your taste buds. Let's explore the international flavors of orange chicken!

Orange Ginger Teriyaki Chicken:

Ingredients:

- 1-pound boneless, skinless chicken thighs, cut into bite-sized pieces
- 1/4 cup orange juice
- 2 tablespoons low-sodium soy sauce
- 1 tablespoon honey
- 1 tablespoon grated orange zest
- 1 tablespoon grated ginger
- 2 cloves garlic, minced
- 1/2 teaspoon sesame oil
- 1/4 teaspoon red pepper flakes (optional)
- Sliced green onions (for garnish)

Instructions:

1. In a bowl, whisk together the orange juice, soy sauce, honey, orange zest, grated ginger, minced garlic, sesame oil, and red pepper flakes (if using) to create the marinade.
2. Add the chicken pieces to the marinade, ensuring they are well coated. Let it marinate in the refrigerator for at least 30 minutes or up to 2 hours.

3. Preheat a grill or grill pan over medium-high heat.
4. Thread the marinated chicken pieces onto skewers or place them directly on the grill.
5. Cook the chicken for about 4-5 minutes per side until it is cooked through and slightly charred.
6. Remove from the grill and let them rest for a few minutes before serving.
7. Garnish with sliced green onions for a fresh and aromatic touch.
8. Serve the orange ginger teriyaki chicken as an Asian-inspired dish, accompanied by steamed rice and stir-fried vegetables for a complete meal.

Orange Chipotle Chicken Tacos:
Ingredients:

- 1-pound boneless, skinless chicken breasts
- 1/4 cup orange juice
- 2 tablespoons lime juice
- 2 tablespoons olive oil
- 2 tablespoons chipotle peppers in adobo sauce, minced
- 2 cloves garlic, minced
- 1 teaspoon grated orange zest
- 1 teaspoon ground cumin
- 1/2 teaspoon smoked paprika
- Salt and pepper, to taste
- Corn tortillas
- Avocado slices
- Chopped cilantro
- Lime wedges (for serving)

Instructions:

1. In a bowl, whisk together the orange juice, lime juice, olive oil, minced chipotle peppers, minced garlic, grated orange zest, ground cumin, smoked paprika, salt, and pepper to create the marinade.
2. Place the chicken breasts in a resealable plastic bag and pour the marinade over them. Seal the bag and massage it gently to ensure the chicken is well coated. Let it marinate in the refrigerator for at least 1 hour or overnight for maximum flavor.
3. Preheat a grill or grill pan over medium-high heat.
4. Remove the chicken from the marinade, discarding any excess marinade.
5. Grill the chicken breasts for about 6-8 minutes per side until they are cooked through and have nice grill marks.

6. Remove from the grill and let them rest for a few minutes before slicing into thin strips.
7. Heat the corn tortillas in a dry skillet over medium heat until warm and pliable.
8. Fill each tortilla with the sliced orange chipotle chicken.
9. Top with avocado slices and chopped cilantro.
10. Serve the orange chipotle chicken tacos as a zesty and flavorful Mexican-inspired dish. Squeeze fresh lime juice over the tacos for an extra burst of citrusy goodness.

Orange and Olive Chicken Tagine:
Ingredients:

- 2 pounds bone-in, skin-on chicken thighs
- 1 tablespoon olive oil
- 1 onion, finely chopped
- 2 cloves garlic, minced
- 1 teaspoon ground cumin
- 1 teaspoon ground coriander
- 1 teaspoon ground turmeric
- 1/2 teaspoon ground cinnamon
- 1/2 teaspoon ground ginger
- 1 cup orange juice
- 1 cup low-sodium chicken broth
- 1 cup pitted green olives
- 1/4 cup chopped dried apricots
- 1 tablespoon honey
- 1 tablespoon grated orange zest
- Salt and pepper, to taste
- Fresh parsley (for garnish)
- Cooked couscous (for serving)

Instructions:

1. Heat the olive oil in a large skillet or tagine over medium heat.
2. Season the chicken thighs with salt and pepper, then brown them in the skillet on both sides. Remove the chicken from the skillet and set aside.
3. In the same skillet, add the chopped onion and minced garlic. Cook until the onion is translucent and the garlic is fragrant.
4. Add the ground cumin, ground coriander, ground turmeric, ground cinnamon, and ground ginger to the skillet. Stir well to coat the onion and garlic with the spices.

5. Pour in the orange juice and chicken broth, stirring to combine.

6. Return the chicken thighs to the skillet, along with any accumulated juices.

7. Add the pitted green olives, chopped dried apricots, honey, and grated orange zest. Stir to distribute the ingredients evenly.

8. Reduce the heat to low, cover the skillet or tagine, and let it simmer for about 45 minutes, or until the chicken is cooked through and tender.

9. Remove the lid and let the sauce thicken slightly for another 10 minutes.

10. Garnish with fresh parsley for a burst of freshness.

11. Serve the orange and olive chicken tagine over a bed of fluffy cooked couscous for a Moroccan-inspired feast that is both exotic and comforting.

These international orange chicken recipes showcase the versatility and adaptability of this delightful dish. From Asian teriyaki flavors to Mexican-inspired tacos and Moroccan tagine, you can explore a world of culinary delights right in your own kitchen. Embrace the global flavors of orange chicken and let your taste buds embark on a delicious adventure!

Chapter 12: Orange Chicken for Vegetarians and Vegans

In this chapter, we'll cater to the vegetarian and vegan crowd by exploring delicious and satisfying orange chicken recipes that are entirely plant-based. Whether you follow a meatless lifestyle or simply want to incorporate more plant-based meals into your diet, these recipes will showcase the versatility of orange chicken flavors without the use of any animal products. Get ready to tantalize your taste buds with these vegetarian and vegan twists on orange chicken!

Orange Tofu Stir-Fry:

Ingredients:

- 1 block extra-firm tofu, drained and pressed
- 1/4 cup orange juice
- 2 tablespoons low-sodium soy sauce
- 2 tablespoons rice vinegar
- 2 tablespoons maple syrup
- 1 tablespoon cornstarch
- 1 tablespoon sesame oil
- 2 cloves garlic, minced
- 1 teaspoon grated orange zest
- 1/2 teaspoon ground ginger
- 1/4 teaspoon red pepper flakes (optional)
- 2 tablespoons vegetable oil
- Assorted stir-fry vegetables (such as bell peppers, broccoli, and snow peas)
- Cooked rice (for serving)

Instructions:

1. Cut the pressed tofu into bite-sized cubes and set aside.
2. In a bowl, whisk together the orange juice, soy sauce, rice vinegar, maple syrup, cornstarch, sesame oil, minced garlic, grated orange zest, ground ginger, and red pepper flakes (if using) to create the sauce.
3. Heat vegetable oil in a large skillet or wok over medium-high heat.
4. Add the tofu cubes to the skillet and cook until they are golden brown and crispy on all sides. Remove the tofu from the skillet and set aside.
5. In the same skillet, add the stir-fry vegetables and cook until they are tender-crisp.
6. Return the tofu to the skillet and pour the orange sauce over the tofu and vegetables. Stir well to coat everything evenly.
7. Cook for a few minutes until the sauce thickens and coats the tofu and vegetables.
8. Remove from heat and serve the orange tofu stir-fry over cooked rice for a complete and satisfying meal.

Orange Cauliflower Bites:
Ingredients:

- 1 small head cauliflower, cut into florets
- 1 cup all-purpose flour (or gluten-free flour for a gluten-free option)
- 1 cup plant-based milk (such as almond milk or soy milk)
- 1/4 cup orange juice
- 2 tablespoons soy sauce
- 2 tablespoons maple syrup
- 1 tablespoon cornstarch
- 1 teaspoon grated orange zest
- 1/2 teaspoon garlic powder
- 1/4 teaspoon ground ginger
- 1/4 teaspoon red pepper flakes (optional)
- Vegetable oil (for frying)
- Sesame seeds (for garnish)
- Sliced green onions (for garnish)

Instructions:

1. In a bowl, whisk together the flour and plant-based milk to create a thick batter.
2. Dip the cauliflower florets into the batter, ensuring they are well coated.
3. Heat vegetable oil in a deep skillet or pot over medium-high heat.
4. Fry the battered cauliflower florets in batches until they are golden brown and crispy. Remove them from the oil and place them on a paper towel-lined plate to drain excess oil.
5. In a separate bowl, whisk together the orange juice, soy sauce, maple syrup, cornstarch, grated orange zest, garlic powder, ground ginger, and red pepper flakes (if using) to create the

sauce.

6. In a large skillet, heat the sauce over medium heat until it thickens and becomes glossy.
7. Add the fried cauliflower florets to the skillet and toss them in the sauce until they are coated evenly.
8. Remove from heat and garnish with sesame seeds and sliced green onions for added flavor and presentation.
9. Serve the orange cauliflower bites as a delicious and crowd-pleasing appetizer or as a main dish alongside steamed rice or quinoa.

These vegetarian and vegan orange chicken recipes prove that you don't need meat to enjoy the mouthwatering flavors of this beloved dish. From tofu stir-fry to crispy cauliflower bites, these plant-based alternatives will satisfy your cravings while nourishing your body with wholesome ingredients. Embrace the world of vegetarian and vegan orange chicken and discover new and exciting flavors!

Chapter 13: Orange Chicken Salads and Bowls

In this chapter, we'll explore refreshing and vibrant orange chicken salads and bowls that are perfect for light and healthy meals. Packed with colorful vegetables, protein-rich chicken, and a zesty orange dressing, these recipes will provide a satisfying and nutritious dining experience. Get ready to indulge in the flavors of orange chicken in a fresh and wholesome way!

Orange Chicken Quinoa Salad:

Ingredients:

- 1 cup cooked quinoa
- 1 cup cooked and shredded chicken breast
- 1/2 cup diced bell peppers (assorted colors)
- 1/2 cup diced cucumber
- 1/4 cup thinly sliced red onion
- 1/4 cup chopped fresh cilantro
- 1/4 cup chopped toasted almonds
- 2 tablespoons orange juice
- 1 tablespoon olive oil
- 1 tablespoon honey
- 1 teaspoon grated orange zest
- Salt and pepper, to taste

Instructions:

1. In a large bowl, combine the cooked quinoa, shredded chicken breast, diced bell peppers, diced cucumber, sliced red onion, chopped fresh cilantro, and chopped toasted almonds.
2. In a separate small bowl, whisk together the orange juice, olive oil, honey, grated orange zest, salt, and pepper to create the dressing.
3. Pour the dressing over the quinoa mixture and toss everything together until well coated.
4. Adjust the seasoning if needed.
5. Serve the orange chicken quinoa salad chilled or at room temperature as a satisfying and nutritious meal on its own or as a side dish.

Orange Chicken Buddha Bowl:
Ingredients:

- 1 cup cooked brown rice or quinoa
- 1 cup cooked and sliced chicken breast
- 1 cup mixed salad greens
- 1/2 cup spiralized carrots
- 1/2 cup spiralized zucchini
- 1/2 cup sliced avocado
- 1/4 cup edamame beans
- 1/4 cup sliced radishes
- 2 tablespoons orange juice
- 1 tablespoon soy sauce
- 1 tablespoon rice vinegar
- 1 tablespoon sesame oil
- 1 teaspoon grated orange zest
- 1/2 teaspoon grated ginger
- Sesame seeds (for garnish)

Instructions:

1. In a bowl or plate, arrange the cooked brown rice or quinoa as the base of the Buddha bowl.
2. Add the sliced chicken breast, mixed salad greens, spiralized carrots, spiralized zucchini, sliced avocado, edamame beans, and sliced radishes on top of the rice or quinoa.
3. In a small bowl, whisk together the orange juice, soy sauce, rice vinegar, sesame oil, grated orange zest, and grated ginger to create the dressing.
4. Drizzle the dressing over the Buddha bowl.
5. Garnish with sesame seeds for added texture and flavor.
6. Serve the orange chicken Buddha bowl as a nourishing and well-balanced meal that combines fresh vegetables, protein, and

the tangy essence of orange chicken.

These orange chicken salads and bowls offer a delightful combination of flavors, textures, and nutrients. Whether you prefer the nuttiness of quinoa or the wholesomeness of brown rice, these recipes allow you to enjoy the vibrant flavors of orange chicken in a light and refreshing way. Indulge in the goodness of these salads and bowls for a satisfying and nutritious dining experience.

Chapter 14: Orange Chicken Wraps and Sandwiches

In this chapter, we'll dive into the world of portable and delicious orange chicken wraps and sandwiches. These handheld delights are perfect for a quick lunch, on-the-go meal, or a satisfying snack. With a combination of tender orange chicken, fresh vegetables, and flavorful sauces, these recipes will take your taste buds on a flavorful journey. Get ready to wrap and roll with these delightful orange chicken creations!

Orange Chicken Lettuce Wraps:

Ingredients:

- 1 cup cooked and shredded chicken breast
- 1/2 cup diced bell peppers (assorted colors)
- 1/4 cup grated carrots
- 1/4 cup chopped water chestnuts
- 2 tablespoons chopped green onions
- 2 tablespoons hoisin sauce
- 1 tablespoon soy sauce
- 1 tablespoon rice vinegar
- 1 tablespoon orange juice
- Butter lettuce leaves (or any other lettuce leaves of your choice)

Instructions:

1. In a bowl, combine the shredded chicken breast, diced bell peppers, grated carrots, chopped water chestnuts, and chopped green onions.
2. In a separate small bowl, whisk together the hoisin sauce, soy sauce, rice vinegar, and orange juice to create the sauce.
3. Pour the sauce over the chicken and vegetable mixture, tossing to coat everything evenly.

4. Take a lettuce leaf and spoon a generous amount of the orange chicken filling onto it.
5. Roll the lettuce leaf, securing the filling inside like a wrap.
6. Repeat with the remaining lettuce leaves and filling.
7. Serve the orange chicken lettuce wraps as a light and flavorful meal or as an appetizer for sharing.

Orange Chicken Banh Mi Sandwich:
Ingredients:

- 1 French baguette, cut into individual sandwich-sized pieces
- 1 cup cooked and sliced chicken breast
- 1/4 cup sliced cucumber
- 1/4 cup pickled carrots and daikon radish
- 2 tablespoons chopped fresh cilantro
- 2 tablespoons mayonnaise
- 1 tablespoon Sriracha sauce
- 1 tablespoon orange juice
- Salt and pepper, to taste

Instructions:

1. In a small bowl, mix the mayonnaise, Sriracha sauce, orange juice, salt, and pepper to create the sauce.
2. Slice the baguette pieces horizontally, but not all the way through, creating a pocket for the filling.
3. Spread the sauce inside the baguette.
4. Layer the sliced chicken breast, sliced cucumber, pickled carrots and daikon radish, and chopped fresh cilantro inside the baguette.
5. Press the sandwich gently to compact the filling.
6. Serve the orange chicken Banh Mi sandwich as a delicious and satisfying meal that combines the flavors of tangy orange chicken with the crispness of vegetables and the crusty goodness of a French baguette.

These orange chicken wraps and sandwiches offer a convenient and flavorful way to enjoy the irresistible combination of tender chicken, zesty orange flavors, and fresh ingredients. Whether you prefer the refreshing crunch of lettuce wraps or the hearty satisfaction of a sandwich, these recipes will satisfy your cravings and keep you satisfied on the go. Get ready to wrap it up or take a big bite and savor the deliciousness of these orange chicken creations!

Chapter 15: Orange Chicken Side Dishes

In this chapter, we'll explore a variety of delectable side dishes that perfectly complement the flavors of orange chicken. These side dishes will elevate your meal and provide a balance of textures and flavors to create a complete dining experience. From rice and noodles to roasted vegetables and refreshing salads, these recipes will add a delightful touch to your orange chicken feast.

Ginger Garlic Fried Rice:

Ingredients:

- 2 cups cooked and chilled jasmine rice
- 1 tablespoon vegetable oil
- 2 cloves garlic, minced
- 1 tablespoon grated ginger
- 1 cup mixed vegetables (such as peas, carrots, and corn)
- 2 tablespoons soy sauce
- 1 tablespoon orange juice
- 2 green onions, thinly sliced
- Salt and pepper, to taste

Instructions:

1. Heat the vegetable oil in a large skillet or wok over medium-high heat.
2. Add the minced garlic and grated ginger to the skillet and sauté for a minute until fragrant.
3. Add the mixed vegetables to the skillet and stir-fry until they are tender.
4. Push the vegetables to one side of the skillet and add the chilled jasmine rice to the other side.
5. Break up any clumps of rice and stir-fry for a few minutes to

heat it through.

6. Pour the soy sauce and orange juice over the rice and vegetables, tossing to coat everything evenly.

7. Cook for another minute or two until the flavors are well combined.

8. Season with salt and pepper to taste.

9. Garnish with thinly sliced green onions for added freshness and serve the ginger garlic fried rice alongside your orange chicken for a flavorful and satisfying meal.

Sesame Roasted Vegetables:
Ingredients:

- Assorted vegetables of your choice (such as broccoli, bell peppers, carrots, and snap peas), cut into bite-sized pieces
- 2 tablespoons sesame oil
- 1 tablespoon soy sauce
- 1 tablespoon honey
- 1 tablespoon orange juice
- 1 teaspoon sesame seeds
- Salt and pepper, to taste

Instructions:

1. Preheat the oven to 425°F (220°C) and line a baking sheet with parchment paper.
2. In a bowl, whisk together the sesame oil, soy sauce, honey, orange juice, sesame seeds, salt, and pepper to create the marinade.
3. Place the bite-sized vegetable pieces on the prepared baking sheet.
4. Drizzle the marinade over the vegetables and toss to coat them evenly.
5. Roast the vegetables in the preheated oven for about 15-20 minutes, or until they are tender and slightly caramelized.
6. Remove from the oven and serve the sesame roasted vegetables as a flavorful and colorful side dish alongside your orange chicken.

These side dishes will complement the vibrant flavors of orange chicken and add depth and variety to your meal. From the fragrant ginger garlic fried rice to the sesame-roasted vegetables, these recipes offer a range of textures and flavors that will satisfy your palate. Prepare these side dishes and complete your orange chicken feast with a delightful assortment of accompaniments.

Chapter 16: Orange Chicken Desserts

In this chapter, we'll explore the sweet side of orange chicken with delicious desserts inspired by its flavors. These treats will satisfy your sweet tooth and provide a delightful ending to your orange chicken meals. From cakes and cookies to refreshing citrus sorbets, these recipes will add a touch of sweetness to your culinary journey. Get ready to indulge in these delightful, orange-infused desserts!

Orange Chicken Cupcakes:

Ingredients:

- 1 ½ cups all-purpose flour
- 1 ½ teaspoons baking powder
- ¼ teaspoon salt
- ½ cup unsalted butter, softened
- 1 cup granulated sugar
- 2 large eggs
- 1 teaspoon vanilla extract
- ½ cup orange juice
- 2 tablespoons orange zest
- Orange cream cheese frosting:
- 8 oz cream cheese, softened
- ½ cup unsalted butter, softened
- 4 cups powdered sugar
- 1 teaspoon orange extract
- Orange food coloring (optional)
- Orange zest (for garnish)

Instructions:

1. Preheat the oven to 350°F (175°C) and line a muffin tin with cupcake liners.

2. In a medium bowl, whisk together the flour, baking powder, and salt.

3. In a separate large bowl, cream together the softened butter and granulated sugar until light and fluffy.

4. Add the eggs one at a time, beating well after each addition.

5. Stir in the vanilla extract, orange juice, and orange zest.

6. Gradually add the dry ingredients to the wet ingredients, mixing until just combined.

7. Fill each cupcake liner about two-thirds full with the batter.

8. Bake for 18-20 minutes, or until a toothpick inserted into the center of a cupcake comes out clean.

9. Remove from the oven and let the cupcakes cool completely on a wire rack.

10. Meanwhile, prepare the orange cream cheese frosting by creaming together the softened cream cheese and butter in a bowl.

11. Gradually add the powdered sugar and orange extract, mixing until smooth and creamy.

12. If desired, add a few drops of orange food coloring for a vibrant orange hue.

13. Once the cupcakes are completely cooled, frost them with the orange cream cheese frosting.

14. Garnish with orange zest for a pop of color and citrus aroma.

15. Serve the orange chicken cupcakes as a delightful and unique dessert that combines the flavors of orange chicken with the indulgence of a moist and fluffy cupcake.

Orange Chicken Sorbet:
Ingredients:

- 2 cups freshly squeezed orange juice
- 1 cup water
- ½ cup granulated sugar
- 1 tablespoon orange zest
- 1 tablespoon lemon juice

Instructions:

1. In a saucepan, combine the orange juice, water, granulated sugar, orange zest, and lemon juice.
2. Bring the mixture to a boil over medium heat, stirring until the sugar has dissolved.
3. Reduce the heat and let the mixture simmer for about 5 minutes to allow the flavors to meld.
4. Remove from heat and let the mixture cool to room temperature.
5. Once cooled, transfer the mixture to a blender or food processor and blend until smooth.
6. Pour the mixture into a shallow, freezer-safe container.
7. Place the container in the freezer and let it chill for 1-2 hours.
8. After 1-2 hours, remove the container from the freezer and use a fork to scrape and stir the partially frozen mixture.
9. Return the container to the freezer and repeat the scraping and stirring process every 30 minutes for about 3-4 hours, or until the sorbet reaches the desired consistency.
10. Once the sorbet is firm and scoopable, it is ready to be served.
11. Scoop the orange chicken sorbet into bowls or cones and enjoy its refreshing and citrusy flavors.

These desserts offer a unique twist to traditional orange chicken flavors, allowing you to indulge in sweet treats inspired by its tangy essence. Whether you choose to savor the moist and citrusy orange chicken cupcakes or cool down with a refreshing orange chicken sorbet, these desserts will provide a delightful ending to your orange chicken culinary adventure. Treat yourself and your loved ones to these sweet delights and satisfy your cravings for something sweet and citrusy!

Chapter 17: Orange Chicken Beverages

In this chapter, we'll quench your thirst with a selection of refreshing beverages inspired by the flavors of orange chicken. These drinks will complement your meal and provide a delightful burst of citrus to awaken your taste buds. From mocktails and smoothies to infused waters and teas, these recipes will add a zesty twist to your beverage options. Get ready to sip and savor these tantalizing orange chicken-inspired drinks!

Orange Chicken Mocktail:

Ingredients:

- 1 cup orange juice
- ½ cup pineapple juice
- 2 tablespoons lime juice
- 2 tablespoons simple syrup
- Splash of grenadine
- Orange slices and mint leaves (for garnish)
- Ice cubes

Instructions:

1. Fill a cocktail shaker with ice cubes.
2. Add the orange juice, pineapple juice, lime juice, simple syrup, and a splash of grenadine to the shaker.
3. Shake vigorously to combine the ingredients and chill the mocktail.
4. Strain the mocktail into a glass filled with ice cubes.
5. Garnish with orange slices and mint leaves for a fresh and vibrant touch.
6. Serve the orange chicken mocktail as a non-alcoholic beverage that captures the flavors of orange chicken in a refreshing and tangy drink.

Citrus Infused Water:
Ingredients:

- 2 oranges, thinly sliced
- 1 lemon, thinly sliced
- 1 lime, thinly sliced
- Fresh mint leaves
- Water
- Ice cubes

Instructions:

1. In a pitcher, combine the thinly sliced oranges, lemon, and lime.
2. Add a handful of fresh mint leaves to the pitcher.
3. Fill the pitcher with water and stir gently to release the flavors.
4. Place the pitcher in the refrigerator and let it infuse for at least 1 hour, or preferably overnight.
5. When ready to serve, fill glasses with ice cubes and pour the citrus-infused water over the ice.
6. Garnish with additional citrus slices and mint leaves, if desired.
7. Sip and enjoy the refreshing and hydrating flavors of this citrus-infused water, which pairs perfectly with your orange chicken feast.

These beverages provide a delightful way to enhance your orange chicken dining experience. Whether you choose the zesty and vibrant orange chicken mocktail or opt for the refreshing and invigorating citrus-infused water, these drinks will quench your thirst and complement the flavors of your meal. Raise a glass and toast to the delicious combination of orange and chicken in these tantalizing beverages!

Chapter 18: Orange Chicken for Special Occasions

In this chapter, we'll explore how to elevate your orange chicken dishes for special occasions and gatherings. These recipes will add a touch of elegance and sophistication to your dining experience, making your meal memorable and extraordinary. From appetizers and main courses to desserts and cocktails, these special occasion orange chicken creations will impress your guests and create lasting culinary memories.

Orange Glazed Shrimp Skewers:

Ingredients:

- 1-pound large shrimp, peeled and deveined
- ¼ cup orange marmalade
- 2 tablespoons soy sauce
- 1 tablespoon orange juice
- 1 tablespoon grated ginger
- 1 garlic clove, minced
- 2 tablespoons chopped fresh cilantro (for garnish)
- Wooden skewers, soaked in water

Instructions:

1. Preheat the grill to medium-high heat.
2. In a small bowl, whisk together the orange marmalade, soy sauce, orange juice, grated ginger, and minced garlic to create the glaze.
3. Thread the shrimp onto the soaked wooden skewers.
4. Brush the shrimp skewers generously with the orange glaze.
5. Grill the skewers for 2-3 minutes on each side, or until the shrimp is cooked through and opaque.
6. Remove from the grill and transfer the shrimp skewers to a

serving platter.

7. Garnish with chopped fresh cilantro for added freshness and presentation.

8.

9. Serve the orange glazed shrimp skewers as an elegant and flavorful appetizer for your special occasion.

Orange Chicken Ravioli with Brown Butter Sauce:
Ingredients:

- 1 package store-bought wonton or dumpling wrappers
- 1 cup cooked and shredded chicken breast
- ¼ cup cream cheese
- 2 tablespoons orange marmalade
- 1 tablespoon chopped fresh parsley
- Salt and pepper, to taste
- 4 tablespoons unsalted butter
- 1 tablespoon fresh lemon juice
- Grated Parmesan cheese (for garnish)

Instructions:

1. In a bowl, combine the cooked and shredded chicken breast, cream cheese, orange marmalade, chopped fresh parsley, salt, and pepper.
2. Place a small amount of the chicken mixture onto each wonton or dumpling wrapper.
3. Moisten the edges of the wrappers with water and fold them over to create half-moon shapes, pressing the edges to seal.
4. Bring a large pot of salted water to a boil.
5. Carefully drop the ravioli into the boiling water and cook until they float to the surface, usually about 3-4 minutes.
6. While the ravioli is cooking, melt the butter in a skillet over medium heat.
7. Continue cooking the butter until it turns golden brown and develops a nutty aroma, stirring occasionally.
8. Once the butter is browned, remove the skillet from heat and stir in the fresh lemon juice.
9. Drain the cooked ravioli and transfer them to individual serving plates.

10. Drizzle the brown butter sauce over the ravioli and garnish with grated Parmesan cheese.

11. Serve the orange chicken ravioli with brown butter sauce as a sophisticated and satisfying main course for your special occasion.

These special occasion orange chicken recipes will add elegance and refinement to your dining table. Whether you serve the succulent orange glazed shrimp skewers as an appetizer or present the delicate and flavorful orange chicken ravioli as a main course, these dishes will leave a lasting impression on your guests. Prepare these recipes with love and attention to detail and celebrate your special occasions with the enchanting flavors of orange chicken.

Chapter 19: Orange Chicken Fusion Cuisine

In this chapter, we'll embark on a culinary journey that combines the flavors of orange chicken with other cuisines from around the world. These fusion recipes will take your taste buds on an exciting adventure, offering a delightful blend of flavors, spices, and techniques. From Mexican-inspired tacos to Asian-inspired stir-fry, these dishes will introduce a whole new dimension to your orange chicken repertoire.

Orange Chicken Tacos:

Ingredients:

- 1-pound boneless, skinless chicken breasts, cut into strips
- ½ cup orange chicken sauce (recipe provided in Chapter 3)
- 8 small flour tortillas
- Shredded lettuce
- Diced tomatoes
- Sliced avocado
- Chopped cilantro
- Lime wedges (for garnish)

Instructions:

1. In a skillet over medium heat, cook the chicken strips until they are cooked through and golden brown.
2. Pour the orange chicken sauce over the cooked chicken and stir to coat.
3. Warm the flour tortillas in a dry skillet or in the oven.
4. Fill each tortilla with a portion of the orange chicken, shredded lettuce, diced tomatoes, sliced avocado, and chopped cilantro.
5. Squeeze fresh lime juice over the taco fillings for added brightness.

6. Serve the orange chicken tacos as a fusion twist on traditional Mexican flavors, combining the tangy orange chicken with fresh and vibrant toppings.

Orange Chicken Stir-Fry with Bok Choy:
Ingredients:

- 1-pound boneless, skinless chicken thighs, cut into bite-sized pieces
- 2 tablespoons vegetable oil
- 3 cloves garlic, minced
- 1 tablespoon grated ginger
- 1 bunch Bok choy, trimmed and sliced
- ½ cup orange chicken sauce (recipe provided in Chapter 3)
- Cooked rice, for serving
- Sesame seeds (for garnish)

Instructions:

1. Heat the vegetable oil in a wok or large skillet over high heat.
2. Add the minced garlic and grated ginger to the hot oil and stir-fry for about 30 seconds until fragrant.
3. Add the chicken pieces to the wok and stir-fry until they are browned and cooked through.
4. Push the chicken to one side of the wok and add the sliced bok choy to the other side.
5. Stir-fry the bok choy for a few minutes until it begins to wilt.
6. Pour the orange chicken sauce over the chicken and bok choy.
7. Stir-fry for an additional minute to coat the ingredients evenly.
8. Remove from heat and serve the orange chicken stir-fry over cooked rice.
9. Garnish with sesame seeds for added texture and nuttiness.
10. Enjoy the fusion of flavors as the orange chicken combines with the crispness of Bok choy in this delicious stir-fry.

These fusion recipes bring together the vibrant and tangy flavors of orange chicken with culinary influences from different parts of the world. Whether you savor the orange chicken tacos, combining the zestiness of orange chicken with the freshness of Mexican toppings, or indulge in the orange chicken stir-fry with Bok choy, blending the tangy orange sauce with Asian-inspired ingredients, these dishes will ignite your taste buds and open up a world of fusion flavors. Embrace the excitement of combining cuisines and enjoy the delightful harmony of these fusion creations.

Chapter 20: Orange Chicken Leftover Makeovers

In this final chapter, we'll show you how to transform your leftover orange chicken into exciting and delicious new meals. Waste not, want not! Instead of letting your leftovers go to waste, repurpose them into creative dishes that will surprise and delight your taste buds. These recipes will give your leftover orange chicken a fresh new lease of life, ensuring that every last bite is enjoyed to the fullest.

Orange Chicken Fried Rice:

Ingredients:

- 2 cups cooked rice
- 1 cup leftover orange chicken, shredded
- 1 cup mixed vegetables (carrots, peas, corn)
- 2 tablespoons soy sauce
- 1 tablespoon sesame oil
- 2 eggs, lightly beaten
- Green onions, chopped (for garnish)

Instructions:

1. Heat a tablespoon of oil in a large skillet or wok over medium heat.
2. Add the mixed vegetables to the skillet and stir-fry until they are tender.
3. Push the vegetables to one side of the skillet and add the beaten eggs to the other side.
4. Scramble the eggs until they are fully cooked and then mix them together with the vegetables.
5. Add the cooked rice, shredded leftover orange chicken, soy sauce, and sesame oil to the skillet.

6. Stir-fry everything together for a few minutes until well combined and heated through.
7. Remove from heat and garnish with chopped green onions.
8. Serve the orange chicken fried rice as a satisfying and flavorful meal that repurposes your leftover orange chicken into a new and exciting dish.

Orange Chicken Salad Wraps:
Ingredients:

- 2 cups leftover orange chicken, shredded
- 4 large lettuce leaves
- ½ cup diced bell peppers
- ½ cup diced cucumbers
- ¼ cup sliced red onions
- 2 tablespoons chopped fresh cilantro
- 2 tablespoons orange chicken sauce (recipe provided in Chapter 3)
- Lime wedges (for serving)

Instructions:

1. In a bowl, combine the shredded leftover orange chicken with the diced bell peppers, cucumbers, red onions, and chopped fresh cilantro.
2. Drizzle the orange chicken sauce over the mixture and toss to coat.
3. Take a lettuce leaf and spoon some of the orange chicken salad onto it.
4. Roll up the lettuce leaf to create a wrap, securing it with a toothpick if needed.
5. Repeat with the remaining lettuce leaves and orange chicken salad.
6. Serve the orange chicken salad wraps as a light and refreshing lunch or appetizer.
7. Squeeze fresh lime juice over the wraps for an extra burst of citrus flavor.
8. Enjoy these wraps as a creative way to enjoy your leftover orange chicken.

With these leftover makeovers, you can give your orange chicken a delicious transformation. Whether you reinvent your leftovers into a flavorful orange chicken fried rice or create refreshing orange chicken salad wraps, these recipes will breathe new life into your remaining orange chicken. Say goodbye to boring leftovers and say hello to exciting and tasty new meals!

Conclusion:

Congratulations on completing your culinary journey through the "Orange Chicken Cookbook"! Throughout this book, we've explored a wide range of recipes that showcase the versatile and delightful flavors of orange chicken. From classic and traditional dishes to creative and fusion-inspired creations, you've discovered numerous ways to enjoy the tangy and zesty essence of orange chicken.

In each chapter, we've provided detailed instructions, variations, and tips to ensure your success in the kitchen. Whether you're a beginner cook or a seasoned chef, this cookbook has been designed to cater to all skill levels, making it accessible and enjoyable for everyone.

From appetizers and main courses to side dishes, desserts, and beverages, you've explored the vast possibilities of orange chicken cuisine. You've learned how to create the perfect orange chicken sauce, marinate chicken for maximum flavor, and even repurpose leftovers into exciting new meals. With each recipe, you've discovered the beauty of balancing sweet, tangy, and savory flavors to create memorable dining experiences.

We hope that this cookbook has not only expanded your culinary repertoire but also sparked your creativity in the kitchen. Feel free to experiment with the recipes, make them your own, and adapt them to suit your personal taste preferences.

Remember, cooking is an art, and the joy of cooking lies in the process of creating and sharing delicious meals with loved ones. So gather your family and friends, invite them to savor the flavors of orange chicken, and create lasting memories around the dinner table.

Thank you for joining us on this flavorful adventure. Happy cooking, and may your kitchen be filled with the aroma of orange chicken delights!

Stay tuned for more exciting cookbooks and culinary adventures to come.

Bon appétit!

JOHN AHMAD